CONTENTS

I0797601

Words in the glossary appear in **bold** type the first time they are used in the text.

BEHOLD THE BLADDERWORT!

"Bladderwort" is a pretty weird name for a plant, isn't it? Well, the bladderwort is a pretty strange plant. You likely think of plants as things animals eat. But the bladderwort is a plant that eats animals! And its name is connected to its carnivorous (kar-NIHV-or-us), or meat-eating, habit.

"Wort" is an old word for "plant." "Bladder" means "pouch" or "sack." Those bladders are a deadly feature. They're actually little traps that capture **prey**! You'll discover more about this weird plant inside this book.

SEEDS OF KNOWLEDGE

Like most plants, the bladderwort is also able to make food from sunlight, water, and a gas called carbon dioxide.

World's Weirdest Plants

Bladderworts Have a Vacuum Trap!

By Janey Levy

Gareth Stevens Publishing

Please visit our website, www.garethstevens.com. For a free color catalog of all our high-quality books, call toll free 1-800-542-2595 or fax 1-877-542-2596.

Library of Congress Cataloging-in-Publication Data

Names: Levy, Janey, author.
Title: Bladderworts have a vacuum trap! / Janey Levy.
Description: New York : Gareth Stevens Publishing, [2020] | Series: World's weirdest plants | Includes index. |
Identifiers: LCCN 2019027406 | ISBN 9781538246368 (library binding) | ISBN 9781538246344 (paperback) | ISBN 9781538246351 | ISBN 9781538246375 (ebook)
Subjects: LCSH: Bladderworts–Juvenile literature.
Classification: LCC QK495.L53 L48 2020 | DDC 583/.96–dc23
LC record available at https://lccn.loc.gov/2019027406

First Edition

Published in 2020 by
Gareth Stevens Publishing
111 East 14th Street, Suite 349
New York, NY 10003

Copyright © 2020 Gareth Stevens Publishing

Designer: Katelyn E. Reynolds
Editor: Abby Badach Doyle

Photo credits: Cover, p. 1 Viktor Loki/Shutterstock.com; cover, pp. 1–24 (background) Conny Sjostrom/Shutterstock.com; cover, pp. 1–24 (sign elements) A Sk/Shutterstock.com; p. 5 Luka Hercigonja/Shutterstock.com; p. 7 Quang nguyen vinh/Shutterstock.com; p. 9 © iStockphoto.com/Nastasic; p. 11 Kenraiz Krzysztof Ziarnek/Wikipedia.org; p. 13 BMJ/Shutterstock.com; p. 15 (main) Gerhard Schulz/Oxford Scientific/Getty Images; p. 15 (inset) JIANG TIANMU/Shutterstock.com; p. 17 Kim Taylor/Nature Picture Library/Getty Images; p. 19 Mps197/Shutterstock.com; p. 21 ideation90/Shutterstock.com.

All rights reserved. No part of this book may be reproduced in any form without permission in writing from the publisher, except by a reviewer.

Printed in the United States of America

Some of the images in this book illustrate individuals who are models. The depictions do not imply actual situations or events.

CPSIA compliance information: Batch #CW20GS : For further information contact Gareth Stevens, New York, New York at 1-800-542-2595.

More than 200 different species, or kinds, of bladderworts exist.

WHERE DO THEY GROW?

If you want to see a bladderwort up close, you likely won't have to go far. Bladderworts are found everywhere around the world except for Antarctica. They grow in bodies of fresh water, or water that isn't salty. That includes lakes, rivers, and streams.

Bladderworts also grow in very wet soil, especially places such as bogs. A bog is a type of **wetland** that has wet, sponge-like soil. In fact, bladderworts can survive almost any place that has fresh water for at least part of the year.

SEEDS OF KNOWLEDGE

More than three-quarters of all bladderworts grow in wet soil and are found in **tropical** areas. The rest of all bladderworts grow in bodies of fresh water.

Look at the pretty flowers on these bladderworts. Would you ever guess there's a deadly trap hiding below?

FAMILIAR AND FUNNY PARTS

What does a bladderwort look like? In some ways, it's like other plants you may be familiar with. In other ways, it's quite different.

A bladderwort has a main stem, leaves, and flowers, just like you would expect. But it doesn't have roots. That would seem to be a big problem, since roots take in **nutrients** a plant needs to live and grow. You'll learn more about that later. And a bladderwort also has those weird carnivorous bladders along its leaves.

The Bladderwort

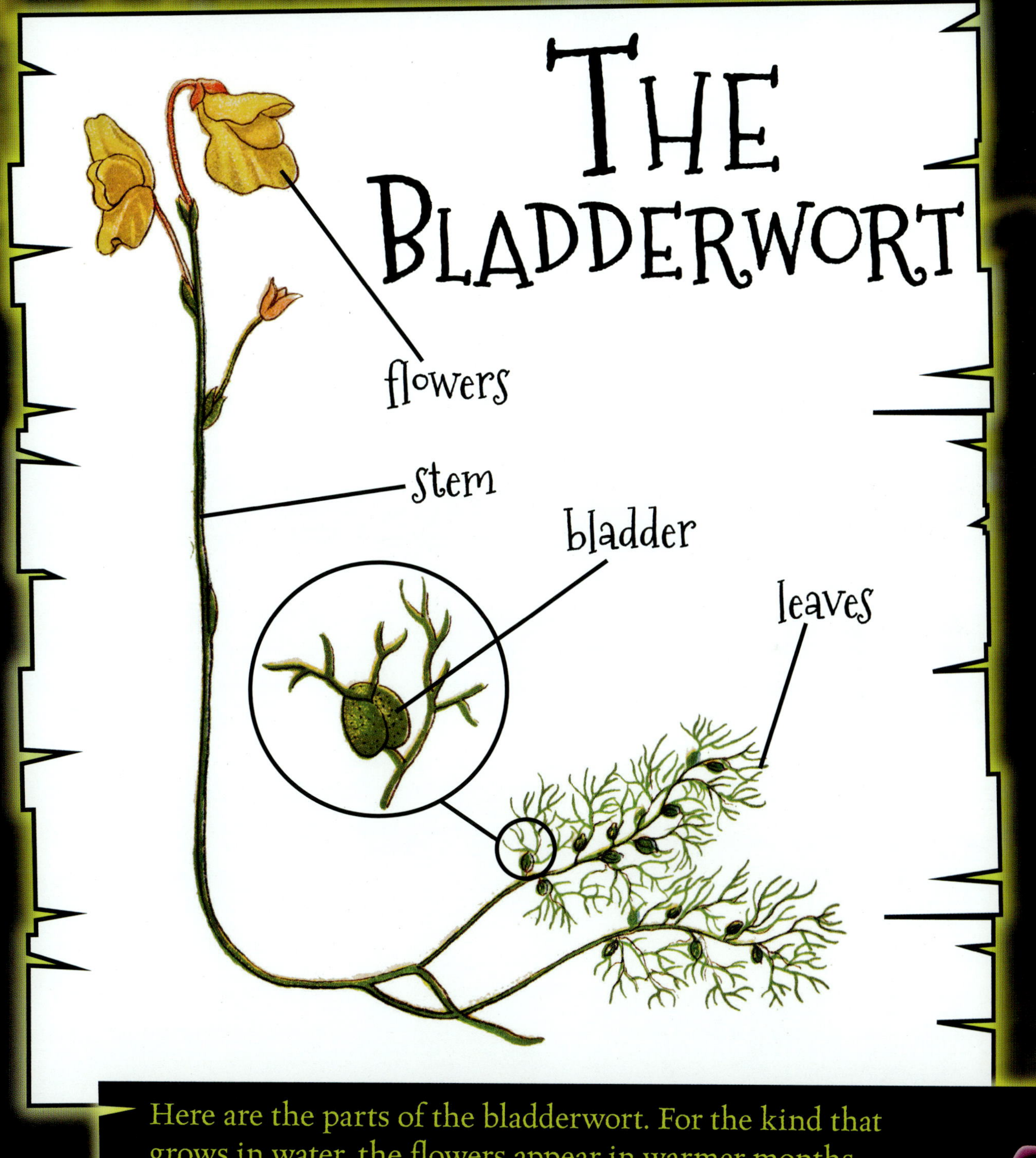

Here are the parts of the bladderwort. For the kind that grows in water, the flowers appear in warmer months.

IN THE BEGINNING

Bladderworts' life story is just as weird as the plants themselves. Like other plants, bladderworts may grow from seeds. But many new bladderworts are created in a different and strange way!

Many bladderworts create ball-shaped turions (TYUHR-ee-uhnz) before winter. These are made of almost-formed leaves, short stems, and lots of **starch**. They sink to the bottom of the body of water and sleep until spring. Then they awaken and start growing. Other new bladderworts can be born from pieces of existing bladderworts!

SEEDS OF KNOWLEDGE

How do bladderworts get spread from one place to another? Scientists believe they're spread by water movement, boats, and birds.

These are turions produced by the common bladderwort. They may not look like much, but they'll produce new life in spring.

WHY DO BLADDERWORTS TRAP PREY?

Your biggest question about bladderworts may be why they have bladders to trap prey. After all, they can make food from sunlight, water, and carbon dioxide like other plants do. But that's not enough.

All plants also need nutrients they usually get from the soil through their roots. But remember—bladderworts don't have roots. Also, they live in places that don't have many nutrients in the soil or water. So to get what they need, they must hunt. Their bladder traps are pretty amazing!

SEEDS OF KNOWLEDGE

Bladder traps are tiny. The smallest traps are 0.008 inch (0.2 mm) wide, or smaller than a grain of sugar. The largest can be 0.48 inch (1.2 cm) wide, or a little bigger than a ladybug.

Bladder traps not only capture prey, but also **digest** it. It can take anywhere from a few hours to several days to digest the prey!

TRICKS OF THE BLADDER TRAPS

How exactly do the bladder traps work? How do they know prey is nearby, and how do they capture the prey?

The trap is round with an opening at one end. A door covers the opening, and tiny hairs stick out around it. The plant pushes water out of the trap, creating a **vacuum** inside it. When a tiny animal or bug touches one of the hairs, the door opens. The vacuum sucks in water and its prey—and then the door snaps shut!

SEEDS OF KNOWLEDGE

The bladder traps don't just sit and wait for prey to come along. They produce a sort of thick slime or goo with sugar in it to draw prey to them.

Bladderworts catch small prey like small worms and fleas.
The traps of each species have a little different size and shape.
lesser bladderwort
common bladderwort

HOW FAST IS FAST?

How long does it take for bladderwort traps to spring open, suck in prey, and snap shut again? Scientists did experiments to find out. It happens so quickly that you need a slow-motion camera to see it!

The whole process, or chain of actions, happens in less than 1 second. Think about this: It takes you about one-tenth of a second to blink your eyes. A bladder trap could open and shut many times in the length it takes you to blink!

SEEDS OF KNOWLEDGE

You might have heard of another meat-eating plant, the Venus flytrap. The bladderwort trap can catch prey 100 times faster than that!

The bladders suck in their prey so quickly that the tiny creatures don't have time to even try to escape.
prey

SECRETS OF THE INSIDE

Prey inside a bladder trap must be digested so the bladderwort can get the nutrients it needs. **Enzymes** and bacteria do the digesting. But scientists who looked at the **microbe** communities inside traps found surprises.

Many bacteria inside the bladderwort produce enzymes to digest plants... not just animals! It turns out bladderworts take in lots of plant matter and **algae** using their traps, too. So, they can get the nutrients they need from this matter by using their plant-digesting bacteria.

SEEDS OF KNOWLEDGE

Some of the microbes in the bladder traps are predators that hunt and eat other microbes inside the traps. This also produces nutrients for the bladderworts.

When they digest plants, the bladders produce a lot of the gas methane, just like cows do. Some people have even compared the bladder traps to tiny cow stomachs!

BENEFICIAL BLADDERWORTS

You might be surprised to learn this weird plant has benefits for the **ecosystem** in which it lives. Its flowers provide nectar for bees. Its bladder traps eat **mosquito** larvae, thus reducing the number of mosquitoes that can bite people.

Bladderworts provide a place for many animals to lay their eggs. Animals such as turtles, salamanders, and bullfrogs hide among the bladderwort's stems and leaves. And some ducks and turtles even eat bladderwort. This strange plant is pretty amazing and important!

SEEDS OF KNOWLEDGE

Mosquitoes carry lots of sicknesses they can pass to people when they bite them. So when bladderworts eat mosquito larvae, they're actually helping prevent the spread of sicknesses!

Bladderworts capture bug larvae, tiny creatures called water fleas, and even tadpoles. In that way, they also help control the population of these creatures in their ecosystem.
golden bladderwort

GLOSSARY

algae: plantlike living things that are mostly found in water

digest: to break down food inside the body so that the body can use it

ecosystem: all the living things in an area

enzyme: matter made in the body that helps certain actions necessary for life to occur

microbe: an extremely small living thing that can only be seen with a microscope

mosquito: a small fly that feeds on the blood of some animals and can spread illness

nutrient: something a living thing needs to grow and stay alive

prey: an animal that is hunted by other animals for food

starch: a type of matter made by and stored in plants

tropical: having to do with the warm parts of Earth near the equator

vacuum: an empty space without any matter in it

wetland: land having high levels of moisture in the soil and usually covered with water at least part of the time

FOR MORE INFORMATION

BOOKS

Loukopoulos, Beatrice. *Plants That Eat Meat*. New York, NY: PowerKids Press, 2019.

Schuh, Mari. *Meat-Eating Plants*. Minneapolis, MN: Pogo, 2019.

Spilsbury, Louise, and Richard Spilsbury. *Killer Plants*. Minneapolis, MN: Bellwether Media, 2017.

WEBSITES

Awesome 8 Carnivorous Plants
kids.nationalgeographic.com/explore/awesome-8-hub/carnivorous-plants /
Learn about eight carnivorous plants—including bladderworts—and see some great photos on this website.

The Ferocious Bladderwort Plant!
www.earthrangers.com/wildwire/plants-2/the-ferocious-bladderwort-plant/
Read up on bladderworts on this site.

Video: World's Fastest Moving Carnivorous Plant
www.sciencemag.org/news/2011/02/video-worlds-fastest-moving-carnivorous-plant
Watch a great video of a bladder on a bladderwort sucking in a tiny animal called a copepod.

Publisher's note to educators and parents: Our editors have carefully reviewed these websites to ensure that they are suitable for students. Many websites change frequently, however, and we cannot guarantee that a site's future contents will continue to meet our high standards of quality and educational value. Be advised that students should be closely supervised whenever they access the internet.

INDEX